T0062959

BIBLE DREAMS TEACH US

Carol J Oschmann

BALBOA.
PRESS
A DIVISION OF HAY HOUSE

Copyright © 2015 Carol J Oschmann.

All rights reserved. No part of this book may be used or reproduced by any means, graphic, electronic, or mechanical, including photocopying, recording, taping or by any information storage retrieval system without the written permission of the publisher except in the case of brief quotations embodied in critical articles and reviews.

THE HOLY BIBLE, NEW INTERNATIONAL VERSION®, NIV® Copyright © 1973, 1978, 1984, 2011 by Biblica, Inc.® Used by permission. All rights reserved worldwide.

Balboa Press books may be ordered through booksellers or by contacting:

Balboa Press
A Division of Hay House
1663 Liberty Drive
Bloomington, IN 47403
www.balboapress.com
1 (877) 407-4847

Because of the dynamic nature of the Internet, any web addresses or links contained in this book may have changed since publication and may no longer be valid. The views expressed in this work are solely those of the author and do not necessarily reflect the views of the publisher, and the publisher hereby disclaims any responsibility for them.

The author of this book does not dispense medical advice or prescribe the use of any technique as a form of treatment for physical, emotional, or medical problems without the advice of a physician, either directly or indirectly. The intent of the author is only to offer information of a general nature to help you in your quest for emotional and spiritual well-being. In the event you use any of the information in this book for yourself, which is your constitutional right, the author and the publisher assume no responsibility for your actions.

Any people depicted in stock imagery provided by Thinkstock are models, and such images are being used for illustrative purposes only. Certain stock imagery © Thinkstock.

Printed in the United States of America.

ISBN: 978-1-4525-9960-1 (sc)
ISBN: 978-1-4525-9959-5 (e)

Balboa Press rev. date: 1/12/2015

Dedicated

To seekers of truth
With thanks to my dream circle
and a special thanks to Katy Zatsick, member
of my dream group, ARCWP (Roman Catholic
Women Priest) and a Carl Jung Society member for
her many incites and additions to this work.

CONTENTS

Part Two

God creating Eve from Adam

INTRODUCTION

The Bible Has Dreams?

The very first happening in one's sleep in the Bible comes in Genesis 2:21-22, "So the Lord God caused the man to fall into a deep sleep; and while he was sleeping, he took one of the man's ribs and closed up the place with flesh. Then the Lord God made a woman from the rib he had taken out of the man." We have been spending a portion of each day, ever since, sleeping. Could God create something wonderful from us also?

The good that God has meant for us often gets buried. Because of all the false impressions we've received over the years about ourselves that have gradually built up in our conscious and subconscious; especially things we're told we are not meant to do ..., we're not a public speaker, we're not to find meaning in our dreams, etc. If God had something wonderful to tell us, He and we would need to delve deep within each of us to bring it to consciousness. It would first be made known to us in our dreams. Are we paying attention?

For many years the people I've met who discussed their dreams with me tell me to expect announcements of new life and new opportunities, or to get a notice that we are headed on the wrong path, there is a better way for us to go. I have found this true.

Did you ever realize how many dreams are in the Bible, and wonder why? The Bible is a teaching book, on that we can all agree. Nowhere does it say not to follow your own dreams, it says the opposite by giving us examples like Jacob, Joseph, Mary, Daniel, a Pharaoh, Solomon, convicts in jail, Moses, shepherds in the field, and many other's dreams. I've read there are one hundred thirty-nine times the word dreams is mentioned in the Bible. We'll take a look at these dreams of the Bible and see what they would mean to us if we had them today.

The people in the Bible knew their dreams were messages from God. They knew dreams were their pathway to direct two-way communication with their creator. By recording these happenings, repeating the stories to others, they have attempted to teach us as well.

Parts of our culture have denied learning through dreams and managed to put a stop to it. The way we think about dreams may be a matter of belief passed down to us from parents, teachers, church, our culture, all supposedly smarter than we are; ... or our own laziness. If your very livelihood depended on catching and heeding your dreams, like the way of life for the people of the Bible, up to the American Indian culture of our more recent past, we would have caught our dreams also.

I can't help but wonder what we have missed by not paying attention to our dreams. Would the disasters we have experienced of late not happened had we all learned to follow our dreams? Would it be easier to discern what path our creator would hope we choose? Is this, perhaps, the ultimate lesson, direct communication with our creator? If you take the Bible seriously, you probably record and follow your dreams like the Biblical characters did.

There are several different kinds of dreams such as anxiety, nightmares, answers to problems, predictive, lucid; to name a few. Reading the various dreams in the Bible, you can see the same kinds of dreams we have each night.

My belief, and I'm not alone, is that this is our own two-way communication connection to our creator. Ever go to sleep with a problem and wake in the morning with the answer? How do you suppose that happened?

We've forgotten how to go to sleep and communicate with our Creator. Therefore, we often forget who we really are. Through listening to our parents, neighbors, teachers and such we often get a false understanding of ourselves. Well-meaning parents want to make us into the best they know how. Perhaps there is a deeper, more meaningful destiny for us. Keeping a dream journal can lead you deeper into who you really are.

Everybody dreams. Watch the movements of the sleeping baby or puppy or kitten. Science has proven that we all dream. In fact, science has proven we would lose our sanity if we did not. What we lose, over the years, is the ability to recall our dream. It works much like a muscle. We lose the power of this muscle if, over the years, we have ignored them or outright said, 'no more dreams.' You can bring dreams back by making them a priority in your life. Repeat constantly to yourself, 'I will remember my dreams.' Read books on the subject, talk about it to whomever you can.

Put a pad and pencil or recorder next to your bed. Write on the pad the date, write 'I will remember my dreams,' then go to sleep. If no dream is remembered, write how you feel or what is going through your head as you wake. Sometimes something will happen during the next day that will make you realize, this was in your dream. Write it down. That night, start with the date again. Take a large drink of water. As you wake to go to the bathroom, wait and think about what was going through you head. You'll remember longer. Soon you'll be getting snippets of dreams or feelings. Write it down as soon as you can because it will disappear. After writing it, forget it, go back to sleep. In the morning, try to understand it. Some are really easy to understand, others deal more with your emotions and need interpreting.

Nightmares are a favorite of mine as they can bring a swift change for the better into your life. As soon as you understand the message God is sending you, the nightmare will not come again. Your life will change for the better. The same goes for recurring dreams. From little recurring dreams, big nightmares grow. Catch the message before it becomes a nightmare! It is like following someone along a path and trying to get his\her attention. Maybe they've won a new car or a million dollars and you need to tell them. You call their name and there is no response. You pick up a pebble and throw it at the persons back. Still no answer, frustrated, you pick up a two by four and hit them over the head. This is God's way, with nightmares, to get your attention. I know I'd be mighty frustrated trying to tell you something that will improve your life and you ignore me. My guess is this must be how God feels with us at times.

Then act on the dream. Write the dream down, draw a picture, tell someone, buy a toy or statue honoring the dream, set it on a shelf of dream symbols. If you can do something, do it. Do you know how many promises you've made to God over the years and not kept? This honoring the dream is all about listening to God in your dreams. As a teenager, I'd stand in church, praying with everyone but saying my own words. "God, please don't let Grandmother know I did ____, I promise not to do it again". Within a short time, I forgot my promise and did it again. The time to bargain with God comes to an end. We have to do all we can to prove our seriousness. God is communicating with us. You can join the ranks of Jacob, Moses and the rest in making that a two-way conversation. God and his angels are waiting.

Metaphorical images such as an egg, and new green plants, or an actual happening, like words and music to a new composition, the solution to a problem, and a leap in research will come to you. Writing your dreams regularly is a small price to pay for the deep truth revealed to you. It is a small price to pay to learn two-way communication with your creator. We bury ideas and opportunities because our pre-conditioning tells us we can't do something. Go to sleep with a pad and pencil next to your bed and when you wake with a dream still active in your brain, write it down. Make use of God reaching inside you to pull out the good that you can do.

God reached inside Adam while he slept and brought forth a new life. What new life lies buried in you? You don't need to understand the dream, just open that dream door and see what new opportunity comes to your waking life. Often you will first need to change a few attitudes. The dreams will lead you. Persistence will pay off. Open that dream door today.

CHAPTER 1

Abram – Abraham

Genesis 11:26 – 25:10

Abraham was best known for leading his son up on the mountain where he had been told by God to sacrifice the boy called Isaac. Abraham totally knew God. He had many conversations with Him, and relied on God's leadership. After Abraham had bound his son, laid him on the stone and raised the knife above Isaac, an angel of the Lord stopped Abraham directing him to a ram that was in the bush behind him to sacrifice instead.

Abraham was also known for fathering the child, Isaac, with his wife Sara when they were both one hundred years old and living until an estimated 175 years old.

Abraham was also a key player in the story of Sodom and Gomorrah. He negotiated with God to save his nephew Lot and his family from the destruction of the two cities.

Although he and God talked easily, there is one story, Genesis 15; 12-15 "As the sun was setting Abram fell into a deep sleep, and a thick and dreadful darkness came over him. Then the Lord said to him, 'Know for certain that your descendants will be strangers in a country not their own, and they will be enslaved and mistreated four

1

hundred years. But I will punish the nation they serve as slaves, and afterward they will come out with great possessions. You, however, will go to your father in peace and be buried at a good old age."

Since my premise is that we can learn something for our own lives from these dreams, that they are more than a retelling of history, I searched my heart. Were there any instances where I would want to receive news like this? We are often given tough times in life and it might be helpful for us to understand why. It may be a part of what scares people away from dream study. Still, the warning of a death of a loved one, for instance, can prepare us, save us from a trauma that could physically hurt us. Or, maybe you will be needed to be the strong one in the group of loved ones grieving.

Were I living in a war torn country, I may be asking God daily, when will this end. What should I be doing? If something terrible were happening to me or my family, I'd like to know why and what I could do about it. This kind of dream has happened to me and to those people with whom I've discussed dreams. Illnesses have been cured by asking our dreams for an answer. Understanding and therefore a decrease in stress can really lighten a load.

Abraham traveled. In Genesis chapter 20:3, is the story of how he passed off his wife as his sister to save his family from a king he feared. The King of Gerar took Sarah, as she was a beauty. That night, in the Kings dreams, "God came to Abimelech in a dream one night and said to him, 'You are as good as dead because of the woman you have taken; she is a married woman." God told him the truth of the lie and why. God promised if Sarah was returned to Abram and no harm came to any of them, no harm would come to the Kingdom of Gerar either.

The King of Gerar was on the wrong path and receiving information about Sarah and Abraham in his dream helped to smooth out the lives of Sarah, Abraham and the king. You can also receive information to pass on to help others smooth out their lives, help them make a decision, or go on a different path, and help yourself at the same time. The King of Gerar, Abraham, and Sarah

2

all benefitted from his dream, first by not making a huge mistake, second, by exchanging many friendship gifts of food, stock and land, and lastly, finding an understanding of each other.

The King of Gerar made a connection with the people in his dream.

When I have a person I know in my dream, I will drop them a letter or make a phone call and let them know what I dreamed. Unless I know this person well, I often pass the dream off as if I'm joking – although I am not. Once, the deceased father of the storekeeper in my small town was in my dream discussing the abilities of his son. He could be president if he wanted to. I wrote the dream and sent it to this man. I got a phone call from him thanking me and telling me he was on the verge of a huge change in his life and had wondered if his father would approve. Now, through my dream, he had the approval so important to him and was about to begin a chain of grocery stores. While I knew him, his chain grew to be nine. I was operating a business of my own, at the time, and, after this, this man helped me in my own business several times.

I have come to know dreams of my daughter are almost always about something in her life that she has not yet decided to share with me. So, yes, I believe God and his angels, our angels, work in our dreams, good or bad, to help make our lives better. When my daughter's life is better, my life is better.

Within my current dream group is a lady named Katy who has studied Carl Jung extensively. She quotes him as saying that we carry within our consciousness a connection to the collective unconsciousness. Due to the creation of God that we are, we have access to this collective and therefore have access to all that is, was and ever will be. Abraham (and we) had this connection through his dreams. There is no time in the collective unconscious. We'll hear more from Katy and her Jungian thoughts as we go along.

JACOBS VISION of the LADDER on his way to HARAN.

יהוה

He dreamed and behold a ladder reached to heaven and the Angels ascending and descending on it
Gen. Ch. XXVIII. V. 12.

Jacob's famous ladder dream.

CHAPTER 2

Jacob

Genesis 25:vs1 - 50

Jacob's life was an epic of dreams. He was the grandson of Abraham, the second son of Isaac. Songs have been written about his dreams like "I am climbing Jacob's Ladder." To understand Jacob's dreams, it helps to understand Jacob. The same is with us. When telling a dream in a group, there are many possible interpretations given but the one who had the dream will know exactly when the truth of the dream is mentioned. Therefore, no one else in the group needs to know any more about the dreamer. The dreamer will get that ah-ha feeling, like an awakening, and will probably think, why didn't I think of that? It is like we are too close to the subject to be able to see the truth for ourselves.

Jacob was a twin, his brother was called Esau. While still in the womb, their mother, Rebecca, was told by God, in a dream, that the baby born second (Jacob) would rule over the first; contrary to the culture of the times. I would guess that Isaac, having been almost sacrificed by his father, Abraham, did not have a close relationship with God, he was more of a follower of the culture in which he lived. Although the boys were born within minutes of each other, the technical oldest would inherit everything. Rebecca, like many of us, searched for a closer relationship to her creator but rather than trust God to fulfill His promise, Rebecca set out to do her part to make sure this happened. When her husband, Isaac, lay on his death bed, Rebecca conspired with Jacob to deceive his father. The oldest son, Esau was to go into a now blind Isaac and receive the blessings of the inheritance of all of Isaac's holdings. As it happened, Esau was working in a far field. Rebecca dressed Jacob in sheep skin to imitate Esau's hairy body. The father was deceived and gave the inheritance to Jacob by mistake. Esau was livid and promised to kill Jacob. Rebecca sent Jacob to live with her brother, Laban

On the long trek to the house of Laban, Jacob prepared to spend one of many nights in the endless wilderness, as told in Genesis 28:vs12-13. "He had a dream in which he saw a stairway resting on the earth, with its top reaching to heaven, and the angels of God were ascending and descending on it. There above it stood the Lord."

This is another message for us all. Jacob honored God for the vision by building a monument to Him in that spot. Not because of this story but, similarly, it has always been my habit to try to find a way to honor God for each dream. If I could find a change to make in my life, my way of thinking, I would do it. If there was something I could draw or buy that represented something in the dream, I would do it. I'd spent so many years making promises to God and not following through; I felt I needed to keep declaring my intent to follow his message.

The other lesson is the sight of the angels coming down to us and returning to heaven, our connection with our creator. We must not miss out on the wisdom our angels, guides and other loved ones bring to us. I've come to know that they know everything about us and want the best for us still.

His mother had been told Jacob was special but still Jacob suffered. He was thrown out of his home, left his beloved mother and traveled across all kinds of land, hoping he'd find his uncle, Laban, whom he'd never met. Also he worried if his uncle would give him a home. He finally came upon a well and the most beautiful girl he had ever seen. He immediately fell in love. Upon inquiring if she knew of a man named Laban, he learned she was Laban's daughter and followed her home. Laban said Jacob could stay and work for seven years at which time he and Rachel could be married, even though she was the younger of two daughters.

Jacob worked diligently for seven years, the wedding took place but when the bride was unmasked, it was not Rachel but her sister, Leah. Jacob had been tricked. Laban then said, if you stay seven more years, you may also marry Rachel. Jacob worked hard, grew himself a herd of cattle, sheep and other livestock to be proud of. So wonderful were they that Laban became jealous and accused Jacob of stealing from him. Jacob married Rachel, took his holdings and left Laban's land.

Jacob, in Genesis 31, vs 10-13, was being cheated at every turn by his father-in-law, Laban. Laban was jealous of Jacobs success in raising not only striped and spotted goats and sheep but jealous of his increasing family and servants as well. Laban was making Jacob's life miserable. God came in a dream during breeding season, while Jacob slept in a field with his herd. Jacob tells the dream. "In breeding season I once had a dream in which I looked up and saw that the male goats mating with the flock were streaked, speckled or spotted. The angel of God said to me in the dream, 'Jacob.' I answered, 'here I am.' And He said 'Look up and see all the male goats mating with the flock are streaked, speckled or spotted, for I have seen all what Laban has been doing to you. I am the God of Bethel, where you anointed a pillar and where you made a vow to me. Now leave this land at once and go back to your native land.'

With the negative atmosphere, the constant disagreements, Laban was keeping Jacob from his destiny. In his dreams and in his life, God was compensating Jacob for his troubles by showing him where, when, and how to proceed with his life. But, you ask, would he give me a place to live, a domain to be the master of? We don't know how many miracles God and his angels are inclined to grant. My thoughts are that it depends on what He perceives as His true need of us. Make yourself available through your dreams and meditations.

God desires our spiritual growth, not increased material possessions. If something is necessary for our spiritual-emotional growth, God will provide it. We may judge the action as negative but God does not. By catching the message, first in our dreams, the negative quality will disappear.

If this were my dream, the mating of the animals might be speaking of something I know how to do but don't get a chance to do. Evidently there was something special about spotted animals and Laban often claimed Jacobs' lambs as his. Is someone stealing my gift from God? Do we talk of our ideas and someone else does them? Sometimes we need freedom and courage to do what we want to do. This is what this dream might be telling me if I had a similar one today.

Jacob headed back to his old home, hoping to impress his mother and brother with his big family and other holdings. Perhaps they would forgive him and let him back in the family. Along the way, riders approached and warned Jacob that his brother was approaching from the other direction with a great army, meaning to kill Jacob. Jacob feared for himself and his family and sent them across the river. While he waited alone to meet his brother, he prayed as he lay down to sleep that night.

In Genesis 32vs 24-30 is the story of Jacob's dream. Jacob was set upon by a man and they wrestled. Jacob was fed up with being the underdog, everyone pushing him around, and fought like he'd never fought before. All night they fought. Finally the man had enough and asked to stop fighting. Jacob said only if the man blessed him with a wonderful gift. The man then revealed that he was an emissary of God, sent to tell Jacob that his name was now Israel because he had wrestled with both man and God and won both times.

Katy would remind us that the 'man' comes from our shadow side, repressed side, often talked of by Jung. Jacob decided to make peace with his shadow side. The story is telling us we can do that also.

Feeling magnanimous, Jacob changed his mind and sent many animals, food and servants to Esau as a peace offering. Esau and Jacob met with open arms of love. Jacob built an alter to God to honor the dream. When we embrace the negative thoughts and feeling within us we heal our inner wounds better and become more whole.

Can you imagine dreaming of wrestling with a monster? It could get very frightening. Talk of nightmares! Jacob got angry with the monster and demanded a gift. Suppose that in your waking life, you are wrestling with a problem that seems to have the best of you, you are at your wits end. In your dreams you get this monster beating you to the ground also. That seems like enough to drive anyone into depression, being forced to accept what you seemingly can't fight. There is a theory that we should turn towards the villain in our nightmares and ask what he wants from us. You can go back into the same dream by closing your eyes and thinking of it.

Instead, know that the monster of your dreams is a part of you, the part of yourself searching for a different outcome. Call it the spark of God inside us all. It wants you to get angry and end the whole thing. Does it mean for you to do something rash? No. It most likely wants to change your view about the path you are on. A change of attitude can make all the difference. Go back into that dream and face the monster and ask, what do you want of me? The real answer will change your outlook, give you a set of answers much better than what you are living. As some wise people say, it is not what they do to me that matters, but rather, how I react to what they do to me.

I have used this dream a few times to illustrate another's dream. To me, Jacob reached the end of his patience, was not about to be taken advantage of and shoved around. Occasionally, I've run into people who have had a similar dream. I ask them to look to where in their life they need to finally take charge. Each time, the dreamer then knew exactly what the dream was about and they took steps to right any wrongs in their life. God, in their dreams, gave them the strength they didn't have before.

From Jacob's dreams I got the idea of honoring each dream, whether I understood it or not. It's like saying, "I'm listening and ready to do whatever you ask." I instinctively knew God would only ask me to do what is right for this world, what is good. The angels ascending and descending the ladders bring the messages we receive in our dreams. What have we missed? It is never too late. As the old saying goes, 'It's better late than never.'

A lady I once counseled about arthritis began talking of a recurring dream she was suffering from regularly. In the dream, a man chased her. She ran clutching her purse. My reaction was to go back into the dream (you can do this) and give him the purse. It is an item men never use. Like them, we can use our pockets if we have to. Go back into the dream, give him the purse and ask him what he wants of you?

She suddenly remembered that her son had built a room onto his house several years ago for her to move into in her old age. She instinctively knew that this was what her dream was about and she was ready to make the move. Later on I received thank you notes from both her and her son. It was all in her dream and the nightmare was over.

My own nightmares were tied to a lack of a feeling of self-worth. I did not realize that was a problem of mine but as I worked with the dreams I gradually changed my opinion of myself, especially of what I could do. I changed my opinion of those who put me down. Before, I had believed them. As I gained wisdom the nightmares disappeared. Besides that, opportunities came that I had no idea I could do. Thank you God!

If you are suffering nightmares at night and stress during your waking hours, your dreams hold the answer to both. Someone a lot older and smarter than you, someone who knows all about you and cares about you anyway, wants the best for you. They (or God) are trying to make your life better, more interesting, healthier, prosperous, fun, etc., etc., etc. We each have a path, and if we are on the wrong path or neglecting our path, we will be unhappy. Dreams (nightmares especially) will bring you step by step in the right direction for you. The reward is wonderful, worth living for.

Jacob's reward was to become the father of the nation known as Israel.

My reward was that I became more self-confident which enabled me to find more suitable employment and also led me into my dream study work.

From Katy we hear that Jung argued that spiritual and emotional work leads to who we really are, or individuation. We can grow into the identity unique to us and dreamed of by God. Like Jacob, God has great plans for each of us.

Joseph being sold by his brothers largely because of his dreams.

CHAPTER 3

Joseph

Joseph was the youngest son of Jacob and also Jacobs' favorite. You may recall the story of Joseph and his coat of many colors that his father had made just for him. His several older brothers were jealous and did not like Joseph very much. This is told in Genesis 37 vs 5. Joseph was a prolific dreamer. In Genesis 37:5, "Joseph had a dream and when he told it to his brothers, they hated him all the more." Verse 8, "His brothers said to him, 'Do you intend to reign over us? And they hated him all the more because of his dream and what he said." Vs. 9 "Then he had another dream, and he told it to his brothers. 'Listen,' he said, 'I had another dream, and this time the sun and moon and eleven stars bowed down to me.'"

When he told his father his dream, his father rebuked him. Lesson one is that we all need someone to talk to about our dreams. Second is to be careful who you chose. There may be times when a journal is all you have to share your dreams.

Some people might be jealous or think you are bragging on something you say you can do and they cannot do it. There is no reason for anyone to be jealous; it is an ability we all have. Its promise depends on the effort you devote to your dreams. So many people have never given a thought to dreams. For this book, I'd like to take each Bible dream as if it came to me, or you, and find other possible meanings that would hold relevance in today's world.

Jungian fan, Katy, tells us the sheaves and the stars are images for the fractured masculine within which must be integrated into Josephs life for him to be whole. Joseph's journey in the rest of his story is to further this integration. For those not familiar with Jung's teachings, we each, male and female, have both masculine and feminine energies. The ideal is to find a balance between them.

If it were my dream, the sheaves may represent a responsibility I have. Perhaps I need to take something in my life and bind it tighter to me, before I lose it. Sheaves are cut from roots I've planted months ago. Maybe it is time to let them go. Maybe it is time to reap reward for all my work. It may simply be a pat on the back as in 'good job.' The sun, moon, and stars bowing to me might be saying the same thing but, I think, also, this is between God and me. I should continue to do the same as I have been doing. Quietly going about my business and await instructions from my dreams.

To continue Joseph's story, his brothers conspired to kill him. They buried him alive in a pit but then hauled him out and sold him to traders headed for Egypt. They marked his famous coat with goat's blood and told his father that he was dead. Joseph became a slave, then ended up in jail. He worked hard in prison, interpreted dreams for others and became friends with his superiors.

During this same time, the King of Egypt's cupbearer and baker were also prisoners because they had displeased the king. They came to be assigned into Joseph's custody. While there, they each had a dream, separate dreams, on the same night.

There are a couple of things to be learned here. First, and most important, is that you don't have to be a special person to have dreams. Some would argue that we are all special. Specialness is not the criteria of whether you remember your dreams or not, or your station in life (because these men were servants and prisoners). Station in life is certainly being shown to us as non-relevant. You are first of all, you, and you will have dreams.

Katy says our unconscious brings forth the images to express the feelings we are experiencing in our waking life, therefore attempting to help us move toward spiritual wholeness.

The second is that they each reported dreams about what they did for a living. We have a saying in dream circles that dreams use what we know, or what we did for a living, to teach us something we don't know. A Postman will dream of sorting mail, going door to door. When you think of all the people on this planet, God and His angels are surely busy and spend a lot of time with our dreams. The dreams use what we've lived, with a small twist, in hopes of convincing us to take a different path, take another look at decisions we are about to make, prepare us for a difficult happening that will actually improve our lives.

Next is the interpretation of the dreams. When they asked Joseph for an interpretation he answered in Gen.40 vs 8, "Do not interpretations belong to God?" In dream groups we tell about what your dream may mean to each of us. You, the dreamer will get that aha feeling when the truth is told. The dream is truly between you and your creator. It helps to have others of like mind to jog our thoughts. Joseph was only guessing but, thanks to his many years of practice, he was right on.

The rest of the dreams of the king's servants talk to us of interpretation. The cupbearers dream told in verse 9 "In my dream I saw a vine in front of me, and on the vine were three branches. As soon as it budded, it blossomed, and its clusters ripened into grapes. Pharaoh's cup was in my hand and I took the grapes, squeezed them into Pharaoh's cup and put the cup in his hand."

Verse 12; "This is what it means," Joseph said to him. "The three branches are three days. Within three days Pharaoh will lift up your head and restore you to your position, and you will put Pharaoh's cup in his hand, just as you used to do when you were his cupbearer." Joseph goes on to try to exact a promise from this man to tell the pharaoh about the dream interpreter but in the long run, he is forgotten for his service.

If anyone should appreciate having a dream interpreted, this man should be him as it is a correct interpretation and relieves him greatly. If it were my dream I might start by drawing a picture of a vine and the three branches of the vine which passes on to a cluster of beautiful flowers that become grapes and ends pouring wine from the grapes into a cup for the Pharaoh. Everything in the dream is alive and growing, prospering, and nourishing. If it were my dream, it might be a promise of good things to come, whether I work for a pharaoh, am a writer, or even the water works department. That opens a new thought. Maybe something is going wrong in the water works department (my emotions) and needs my tender care to clean out unnecessary weeds.

It all depends on the life you are living. The three branches, or three of anything can refer to the trinity, a message from God. I love the opportunity to nourish others, as the healthy grapes would do. Then, again, perhaps I'm being warned of someone in my circle of friends drinking too much. The person having the dream knows the truth by that aha feeling God will give him or her.

Katy reminds us that we are all connected to God. Jung calls this realization of the _Self_ within us. Our growth is dependent on our consciously connecting to the Self, and dreams may show the way for us to do this.

The baker, however has quite a different dream. Genesis 40, vs 16-17 "When the chief baker saw that Joseph had given a favorable interpretation, he said to Joseph, 'I too had a dream: On my head were three baskets of bread. In the top basket were all kinds of baked goods for Pharaoh, but the birds were eating them out of the basket on my head.'"

Again Joseph saw the three items (dead, not growing) holding baked goods that because of his positioning of them on his head allowed birds to eat them, leaving nothing for the Pharaoh. Joseph interpreted that he would be dead in three days, hung from a tree, food for the birds. The baskets hold nothing and perhaps Joseph saw this as the man, himself. We often work with the idea that every person and everything in a dream is a part of us. This baker was an empty basket – dead. The birds were the baker's future. There would be nothing left for the Pharaoh.

If it were anyone else's dream, the empty baskets on the head might be pointing to a life of head more than heart. The birds are very spiritual. The fact that they were trying to feed out of empty baskets, or gathering crumbs, may be telling the dreamer to prepare his spiritual life. His soul, symbolized by the birds may be preparing for a spiritual journey. If it were your dream, look where you might make changes, become a gift to the world.

The Pharaoh would see future nourishment with the cupbearer but not the baker and decided their fates accordingly. Your own death seen in a dream usually means a change is coming, or should come, I've seen my own death many times and I'm still here.

Katy says that Jung taught that we will not dream of our own death directly. The dream of the baker supports the use of images for our death. Katy says she believes it is because our soul, or self, will never die.

Interpreting others dreams is not bad so long as the feeling of truth is left to the dreamer. It is very helpful to the dreamer, and it opens your own mind to several possible truths. God will tell the dreamer when the right one is mentioned. Understanding your dream can bring an end to that kind of dream, it won't become a nightmare, and your life will change for the better. Your path of life will come closer to what it is meant to be, who you were meant to be. If you were that baker, you might have saved your own life by finally turning to the spiritual side of life. Start a conversation with God.

Then in the 41st chapter of Genesis, two years have passed with Joseph in prison in Egypt. The Pharaoh has two dreams in the same night. Asking around, he finally learns of Joseph's ability to interpret dreams and consults with him. Here begins the story of the dream of the seven sleek and fat cows that come out of the river followed by seven ugly, gaunt cows. The Pharaoh wakes, goes back to sleep and dreams of seven heads of grain, healthy and good, followed by seven heads of thin, scorched by the wind, heads of grain.

When God has a message for you and you do not get it the first time, a different story with the same theme will come in future nights, eventually becoming stronger and scarier. If it were my dream, I might worry about my health, about the fact that the things I nourish my body with are failing me. But I do not have the responsibilities of a pharaoh.

Joseph interprets the two dreams as seven years of abundance followed by seven very tough years for the world. The pharaoh sees the wisdom of Joseph's words and puts him in charge of all of Egypt, second to no one except the Pharaoh, himself. Joseph stockpiles the food during the next seven years of plenty and has plenty of food and grain to sell and feed not only to the Egyptians but others as well. Can you see the fulfillment of Joseph's childhood dreams? Later on in the story, his brothers do, indeed, bow down and beg for food from him.

What's to learn from this besides how to manage your assets? People believe Joseph has direct access to God. Joseph has been dealing with dreams since his early childhood while most others, much like today, can't spend the time to learn how. I find in my dream groups that some people have a natural ability and others need to spend time and effort learning to do it. The others do learn to understand the dreams and can become very good at it. So, where does that leave us as far as the belief that God is talking to us goes?

Our creator never meant to lose touch with us. He gave us all the power of dreams. If you believe in the writings of the Bible, you should want to study and learn to understand the emotional and spiritual language of your dreams, as it says in the Bible. Whether it is God speaking directly to us, a committee of loving spirits, our personal angels, or at times all three; we have dreams that tell us all kinds of good things, and they warn us of the bad. Someone older and wiser than us, someone who cares about us and wants the best for us, our health, our finances, our joy; that someone speaks to us in our dreams.

Katy says that God has a part for each unique individual to play in the evolution of human consciousness and spirituality.

We could possibly avoid some of the results of the various disasters if we paid attention to our dreams like Joseph and the Pharaoh did. That is what Genesis 41 is telling us. Some people believe the disasters come to teach us lessons. Some of us learn those lessons, after the fact. Some learn for a while during the turmoil. Few of us continue the humanitarian aspects of life for very long afterward. We go back to thinking and feeling about those less fortunate than ourselves, usually the lesson, the same way as we did before the storm, earthquake, whatever the disaster is.

Perhaps, though, the ultimate lesson is to monitor our dreams for the predictions they bring us. We can begin the clean-up or avoid the disaster before it happens.

Katy says that a physical event always is reflective of an emotional/spiritual change within ourselves. Jacobs emotional/spiritual experience moves him to go to Egypt, a "new foreign" position for he and his family.

Toward the end of Genesis, chapter 46, Joseph had prospered and caused all of Egypt to turn to him for guidance. This included his brothers although they did not recognize him, Joseph knew them immediately. He asked to be reunited with his youngest brother and his beloved father, Jacob, who all these years thought him dead. In verse 2, "And God spoke to Israel (Jacob) in a vision of the night and said, "Jacob, Jacob." Jacob answered "Here I am, he replied." 'I am God, the God of your father; do not fear to go down to Egypt, for I will make you a great nation there."

Jacob loaded all his belongings and people and went.

If you had a dream telling you to do something, would you? We often have dreams but no way of knowing who is talking to us. I try always to honor each dream. If there is a clear direction, I do my best to follow it. My faith tells me God would never tell me to hurt someone or myself. If I get a bad image, I turn it around, look at the opposite of the action. Many wonderful results have come from this. May God bless you likewise.

THE ANGEL APPEARING TO JOSEPH

ΘΕΟΣ

Behold, the Angel of the Lord appeared unto him in a dream, saying, Joseph thou son of David, &c.
Matt.I.20.

Pub by Alex Hogg & Co Paternoster row

Joseph's dream of angel.

CHAPTER 4

Exodus, Leviticus, and Numbers

The next two books of the Bible are free of dreams. The next, Numbers, does not mention them until the twelfth chapter, vs. 6. "Listen to my words; When a prophet of the Lord is among you, I reveal myself to him in visions, I speak to him in dreams. But this is not true of my servant Moses; he is faithful in all my house."

Moses was not a prophet. He is more and has been given many gifts that astonished Moses and the people viewing the action and reading the book, such as turning a walking stick into a snake and the back into a stick. Moses is a strong leader and his reign is filled with new laws. Through the many years of his reign, however, Moses' people were seldom satisfied and the Lord suffered with them, wondered how to handle them?

I find it interesting that in verse 6 he says he will talk to Moses clearly, not in riddles. I've often been frustrated and heard other people express frustration over the need to interpret our dreams. Some dreams come very clear, and at times a clear sentence will come through with directions pertaining to whatever is important in your life. The other dreams come to change our attitude about something. What would it take to get you to go with a second choice, or third you would never have considered? I've been faced with problems, asked God, before going to sleep, which way to go and have a dream about a third choice I'd never thought of. If you believed someone older, wiser and loving wanted to change the way you felt about something, you very well might take a different path. First of all, you need to be open to the advice of your dreams, keep that pad and pen next to your bed so you don't miss a dream.

In a dream, I was told that after this earthly life, I would serve on a committee that gives dreams to people on earth. I worry if I understand human nature enough to have any idea what it would take to change their minds on something. Serving on a committee of souls trying to mold the thoughts and feeling of people on earth brings some comfort. I don't want to miss this chance of service. It is all about seeing a situation from various views. The views could convince the person to choose differently.

When I began my serious dream study, it took only a year to erase rheumatoid arthritis from my blood stream. It took following the dreams as closely as I could. My relationships changed, my vocation certainly changed. I did not grow up wanting to do dream work, I didn't even know what dreams were. I saw in the dreams different ways to see things. My first thoughts, or ego thoughts, did not always suit me after I saw other ways of viewing a situation in my dreams.

Often you think you are simply reliving something that happened in your life. Rev. Jeremy Taylor (an Episcopal dream researcher) told us that the dreams use what you know to teach you what you don't know. Think on that. I had a male friend who was a hospital administrator for most of his adult life. The dreams he related to us in dream group often had him back in that hospital, walking the same halls and rooms. He had to look at the inconsistencies, the twists, compare them to whatever was going on in his life at the moment to find the message. Dreams use what you know to teach you what you don't know. If you delivered mail for a living, this is where your message may be hidden. The dream messengers, the Lord, want you to follow your own truths, make your own choices.

Unlike the people of Moses time, who were asked to follow blindly, most of us have the power of choice.

CHAPTER 5

Deuteronomy 13:1

"If a prophet or one who foretells by dreams, appears among you and announces to you a miraculous sign or wonder, and if the sign or wonder of which he has spoken takes place, and he says, 'Let us follow other gods and let us worship them, you must not listen to the words of that prophet or dreamer."

This is, perhaps, the most misunderstood passage in the Bible. If it weren't for the 139 dreams, the Bible would be very thin. Some people take this to mean to stay away from dreams altogether. Nowhere in the Bible does it say to not follow your own dreams, not listen for your creator's voice. It says the opposite in several places.

This verse has been thrown in my face by people who've heard of it but not taken the time to read the Bible themselves. I went back to the beginning of the Book of Deuteronomy and read every word to get a feel for whatever was going on. Moses, at this point, is reaching the end of his years and must pass his knowledge of the laws onto the leaders taking his place. I can understand his saying something to the affect to get your own messages from God, not an in-between person. Nowhere does it say to not follow your <u>own</u> dreams.

Other Biblical scholars have said this book was translated from Arabic to Spanish by the translator, Jerome, who made a mistake in the word dream. The word was originally to be fortune teller. Jerome is credited with ten mistakes. The Bible has been translated many times, not only to change the language but also to change the meaning as witnessed by the many translations on the market today. The rest of Deuteronomy is about the many laws God passed through Moses, like the Ten Commandments.

After Moses died, Joshua was given command by God. He followed the rules and God helped him conquer a lot of the land the Israelites had been promised. After the reign of Joshua, the people became friendly with the people they had overcome and some began to follow other Gods. This brings us to the book of Judges and the rule of Gideon. Although God spoke directly to Gideon, Gideon was hard to convince that he was really hearing from God. Gideon asked for signs that what he was thinking was truly God. When he was convinced, he often bargained with God.

Katy reminds us that only the dreamer knows the true meaning of the dream, although it may take several dreams to finally get the message across. Katy asks, who is the God of our understanding. She says we each have a unique relationship with our Higher Power. First the dream is for me, about my challenges, choices, and feelings. Dreams arise from my personal unconscious. Secondly, dream images may come from the collective unconscious (the unconscious belonging to the world) bring knowledge of archetypes, such as the father and mother – something we all share and, therefore connections with other people and/or knowledge beyond our conscious understanding of a situation. The dream material must be true for me or otherwise set aside.

God creating light in the world and also
through our understanding.

CHAPTER 6

Judges 7:13

The action is very much similar to the better known story of Sodom and Gomorrah. God needs to weed out the people who do not bring honor to his name. In Sodom and Gomorrah, Abraham is negotiating with God to save a community. "If I can find ten honorable people will you still destroy the community?" The next morning, a group of angels are accosted on their way into town and all deals are off. The towns are wiped out.

In Judges, the story concerns God and Gideon. There is much negotiating as Gideon does not want to go to war with these people. God convinces him to take one trusted person with him and scout the camp during the night. The decision is left up to Gideon, so to speak. In Judges 7:13, "Gideon arrived just as a man (an enemy) was telling a friend his dream. He was saying 'A round loaf of barley bread came tumbling into the Midianite camp. It struck the tent with such a force that the tent overturned and collapsed.' Judge 7:14, "His friend responded,' this can be nothing other than the sword of Gideon, son of Joash, the Israelite. God has given the Midianites and the whole camp into his hands."

Judges 7:15 "When Gideon heard the dream and its interpretation, he worshiped God. He returned to the camp of Israel and called out. 'Get up! The Lord has given the Midianite camp into your hands."

The writers of the bible are proving that God has a hand in everything. We oft times see something familiar. The dream and its interpretation were very familiar to Gideon and he knew when the very same words were repeated through someone else's dream, God was re-emphasizing His message. If I were Gideon, today, I believe I'd be having a feeling of de ja vue.

It happens to most of us some time in our life, that we walk into a room or a situation and feel that we've been there before. Perhaps we've been shown it in our dreams. If this is the way things are supposed to work, if people were to take heed of their dreams, would much of the fighting of this world never happen?

There is a book entitled "The Third Reich of Dreams," written mostly in the 1930s' before the Second World War started. The author, a German lady named Charlotte Beradt, a journalist, was able to gather hundreds of dreams. Often the people to whom she spoke about such things did not even know she was keeping a journal of them. The person who wrote the introduction saw in the telling that the Nazis could reach into our dreams and scare us into submission. Charlotte Beradt escaped to England in 1940 and eventually to the US where she published this book in 1966.

I see something different when I read the book. I see the horror coming to the average German, but I also see a chance to change things. I believe Ms. Beradt did also which would explain her escape to England.

We can know the future from our dreams. It is too bad we lost our belief in this ability for communication with our creator for so long. In my work with dream groups, I find hope as more and more people become interested in learning what their dreams are telling them.

In the beginning of the story of Gideon, it seems as though Gideon is talking directly to God. Why, then, did he not believe him? He believed when he heard another person tell his dream and the interpretation so very similar to what he'd experienced. Then he knew God was God and God was serious. We may be getting messages each night in our dreams and are doubting they are from God.

As for the dream, itself, the ball of barley is rolling down the hill to crush the camp. How would you feel if a huge ball of something were about to run over you and there was no way of getting out of the way? Pretty scary. Are you in the wrong place in life? Bread, to me, means manna which is a gift from God. If you or I had a similar dream, it might very well mean there is something in our life about to be rolled flat to make room for God's purpose. I believe it is a spiritual thing, could be a belief or attitude, because of the word, bread. It would be a warning of change or maybe a gift from God.

CHAPTER 7

1 Samuel

1 Samuel 3:5; (paraphrased) Samuel was born to a woman desperate for a child. During this time, Eli was God's representative and once every year, the people would go to Eli and sacrifice grains and animals. Eli saw this woman (Hannah) crying and praying so he asked God to grant her wish. She became pregnant and gave the boy child to Eli to grow up as a man of God. She had several children after that.

Eli's own sons were thieves, taking from the sacrificial goods brought by the people. One night God called Samuel's name as he slept. Samuel thought it was Eli and ran to him. It happened again. The third time, Eli figured out that God must be calling to Samuel in his dream and told Samuel to go back to sleep and, upon hearing his name called again say "I am Samuel, God, what can I do for you?" 1 Samuel 3vs 11-14 "And the Lord said to Samuel: 'See I am about to do something in Israel that will make the ears of everyone who hears of it tingle. At that time I will carry out against Eli everything I spoke against his family – from beginning to end. For I told him that I would judge his family forever because of the sin he knew about; his sons made themselves contemptible, and he failed to restrain them. Therefore, I swore to the house of Eli, the guilt of Eli's house will never be atoned for by sacrifice or offering."

Samuel was being given a prediction of something to happen against the family who raised him. Is it possible that you might be given a prediction of some awful thing happening in the future to someone you know?

Yes, it happens, but remember, God cares about you and wants to forewarn you to make the shock lesser for you. The worst thing for the health of our bodies is stress. Also, in the case of a death, every group needs one strong person to lean on and you have that chance to be that strong person.

There are few dreams between Genesis and 1 Samuel. We go through the books of Exodus, Leviticus, Numbers, Deuteronomy, Joshua, Judges, and Ruth. In Exodus, Moses warned against dreamers and seers. There are a couple of reasons given by bible scholars as to why Moses is quoted as saying what he did. Some say Jerome, a Bible translator made ten mistakes, my own personal belief is that Moses wanted people to rely on their own connection with God. Nowhere in the Bible does it say not to follow your own dreams.

After his death there was at first a series of kings and then, for a long time, no kings or central leaders. The people who had based their lives on Gods leadership began turning to other kings. In these books of the Bible are a series of wars. Sounds like today in the Middle East.

It pleased me that in 1 Samuel 28, Saul, who had banished all seers and dreamers from his land suddenly saw a need for a medium who could help him get advice from the Lord to save his country. Remind you of the atheist in the foxhole? Many of our own leaders seem to have lost the ability to hear God's voice.

In chapter 28; verse 5-7 it is written; "When Saul saw the Philistine army, he was afraid: terror filled his heart. He inquired of the Lord, but the Lord did not answer him by dreams or Urim or prophets. Saul then said to his attendants, 'find me a woman who is a medium, so I may go and inquire of her."

There is a time when we need God. In verse 15 Samuel says to Saul, 'Why have you disturbed me by bringing me up?' 'I am in great distress,' Saul said. 'The Philistines are fighting against me, and God has turned away from me. He no longer answers me, either by prophets or by dreams. So I have called on you to tell me what to do."

It is not God who turns away from us. It is we who do the turning. We must learn to remember our dreams, keep the doors of communication with God open.

Katy says that Saul was unable to listen to his dreams because it is something we should practice continuously. When we are emotionally and physically stressed, mentally ill, have addictions, we will have to focus on healing. Our dreams may reveal a path for our healing. Because of Saul's circumstances, he could not choose a healthy path forward without knowing how to listen to God in his dreams.

SAUL AND THE WITCH OF ENDOR

יהוה

Saul perceived that it was Samuel, & he
stooped with his face to the ground, &
bowed himself.
1 Samuel ch. 28. v. 14.

Pub. by Hogg & Co. Paternoster row

Saul regrets his edict against dreamers and searches
out the witch known as Endor to dream for him.

CHAPTER 8

1 Kings

Kings continues the history of the time began in 1 Samuel. King David, as he approached his own death, bequeathed the kingdom to his son Solomon. He told Solomon, in 1 kings 2 vs 2 "So be strong, show yourself a man and observe what the Lord your God requires: Walk in his ways, and keep his decrees and commands, his laws, and requirements, as written in the law of Moses, so that you may prosper in all you do."

Solomon did a good job but felt insecure because of his young age. Still he struggled to do what he believed God would ask of him. One night, the Lord appeared to Solomon during a dream, and God said, 'Ask for whatever you want me to give you.' God granted him the wisdom he became known for. In 1 Kings 3, vs 15, "Then Solomon awoke and he realized it had been a dream."

Have you ever gone to sleep with a huge problem that you had no idea the right way to solve? You could do one thing or you could do another, but which was right? Did you wake in the morning with the answer? This happens a lot. Even, sometimes, you were not aware you had a problem but woke with a shift in your path of life clearly in mind and feeling good about it.

We have, in our dream group, a ritual we teach of writing your question for God on a piece of paper, hold it in your hand and pray about it. Tuck it under your pillow and turn out the light; lay your head on your pillow, still praying about it. Go to sleep. Write whatever dreams come to you that night. In the morning, you'll have the answer.

Suppose a friend asks you to dream for him or her. Follow the same procedure. As nature calls, lay still contemplating what had gone through your head just before waking. Write it down as soon as you can. The longer you wait to write, the more of the dream and the answer, you will lose. God and His angels will cloak the answer in a story because it really is not yours to know. The person you are dreaming for will recognize the truth.

In 1Kings 3 vs 5 "At Gibeon the Lord appeared, to Solomon during the night in a dream;" without being called. God does this with us also. He knows what is bothering us before we do. Some questions He has answered has been as simple as "Why can't I not remember my dreams?" I have found that nothing is too simple for an answer to come to us. If it is important to us, it will be answered. Often there is another way of looking at the problem that you might never have considered had you not asked God, a wee bit of the wisdom Solomon received. I found that the mere act of asking will reopen doors between you and God. In my book "God Speak in Dreams" I've recounted several stories of the question and answer type that were either for me or for another person who asked for guidance, and the answers we received.

It is important to honor this dream or set of dreams, in some way. Write it down. If there is a food, I'd either add or delete it from my diet. Draw a picture, start a collection of dream symbols, share the dream with a trusted person. Rewards will come.

Rewards, I have found, will show up in life. Rewards come that set you closer to your true path through life because you're finally turning to God. For instance, as I watched my canvas building equipment being driven away down my street. My heart was heavy as I had failed at this endeavor. Within minutes, the mailman arrived and in his hands was an invitation to write for a sporting magazine. This was a career that lasted for several years and gradually morphed into writing books about dreams and also a young adult fiction, plays, and giving lectures about dreams.

As I said before, God leads you step by step. If you are tuned in to hearing his voice in your dreams you are more likely to have that better life – here on earth.

Also in this story of Solomon's dream, God says in 1Kings 3 vs 11-12 "Since you have asked for this (guidance to help your people), and not for long life or wealth for yourself, nor have asked for the death of your enemies but for discernment in administering justice, I will do what you have asked." In addition, God promised to give what Solomon needed, wisdom, not exactly what he asked for. Who knows better than God what we really need? Sometimes I have been surprised by the superiority of what God gave me, compared to what I thought I wanted or needed.

I wish I had read this and understood the verse long before I asked for lottery numbers. With so many wonderful things that were coming into my life, by the grace of God, I asked before falling asleep for the winning lottery numbers. In a dream, I was given numbers and the next day I played those numbers. I lost. Amazed that my God had left me hanging, I asked the next night, "Why did you give me the wrong numbers?" A voice came before my head hit the pillow, "You have to learn to earn your money."

The directions are right there in your dreams.

Katy would add that there are many gifts within each of our personalities, some have become repressed, now known as our shadow, and wait for us to explore for them. Some gifts have not yet been discovered on our life journey of emotional and spiritual growth. If we face our fears and challenges new gifts will arise for us. Our shadow can be very beneficial to us.

Solomon using his wisdom.

CHAPTER 9

Job 4:13-16

"Amid disquieting dreams in the night, when deep sleep falls on men, fear and trembling seized me and made all my bones shake. A spirit glided past my face, and the hair on my body stood on end. It stopped, but I could not tell what it was. A form stood before my eyes, and I heard a hushed voice."

This came to Job amid all his other problems and questioning of the torments that he (a God fearing man) was suffering. I have had similar dreams or happenings in my life. I've heard other people report the same. If you handle it right, ask God to take them away, it will not happen again. But there may be something worth learning from these spirits.

I had been working steadily with my dreams, God and meditations to get on the path for which I was intended. One night, as I slept, I, too, heard a soft voice. I opened my eyes to see three figures standing at the foot of my bed. Okay, I'm human, and a girl, as if that should make me a member of the weaker sex. I think this apparition would shake anyone to the core. Immediately, I shouted inside myself for God to take this away. They left and have never come back, at least twenty-five years at this point.

The first point being that if you sincerely work with God, God will work with you. One of the big questions the Bible raises is why did Job have to suffer so much? First of all, we are not Job. It seems to me that he was a very negative person. Hopefully, most of us have things we are grateful for and thank God. I was working to get on the path for which God intended me. I do know, from many happenings I experienced during that time, ask and you'll receive. God took the spirits away. Later I'd heard that perhaps they were wise men come to help me on my quest. But I said to take them away and they never came back. Still things improved for me.

Has this happened to others? I believe so. In my prison volunteer program, one young lady told how she had been shot in the head as a child and now wears a false eye. All these years, she's hated to go to sleep because ugly beings want to torture her, tear her apart. I told her my story of telling God to take the beings away and how they disappeared forever. That night, she tried this solution. One of her bunk mates said she had witnessed her yelling at God to take them away. They left. Several weeks later, they were still gone.

Another way to get rid of them comes in a story another inmate and I shared. She told of suffering from nightmares ever since being in prison, about five years. It came about because of her rape and the death of her husband. She was keeping the whole cell block awake with her screams. My feeling was that five years was long enough to suffer and that she should, hopefully, find some other thing, a moment of joy, to erase these memories and their impact.

The next night I was teaching a class on dreams, I talked about the movie, "The Wizard of Oz." We would center on the dog, Toto, the tin man and such, the music, have a good time. Guess what, she was the only one in the room not familiar with the movie. I seemed stuck. We had a couple of visitors, that night, who called themselves biker-babes. We got to joking over which bike was better, the Harley-Davidson or the Honda. My husband owns a Honda. We had some good natured joking during my two hour stay.

The next week, the Spanish lady came in smiling. The guards had woken her because, for once, she was laughing in her sleep. They wanted to know why. She had been dreaming that she was sitting on a motorbike. In her dreams, she caught the joke and was laughing. My assumption of enough time suffering was right. The biker babes (farthest from herself) broke the cycle.

Katy says the Spanish inmate met the "biker babe" energy within and she rode it. She was finally in control, releasing her from the PTSD of rape and death. She could "ride the energy within" and heal.

Maybe the point was about breaking cycles? Faith in God broke my cycle. Finding joy in the things I was learning about communication with God is what broke my cycle of nasty spirits. Perhaps it did for her also.

Job goes on. In chapter 4 verse 20, "between dawn and dusk they (meaning humans) are broken to pieces: unnoticed they perish forever. Verse 21, Are not the cords of their tent pulled up, so they die without wisdom?" It is better to get to know God in your dreams before you die. It is our chance to gain some wisdom. The choice is ours. Wisdom comes in dreams if we work to find it.

There is a whole lot more to be said about nightmares. They come to bring you a message from God and once you understand that message, the nightmare never returns and your life improves. It is too bad Job had to go through what he did and to have the negative attitude that he did. At the end of his story, Job did figure it out.

Katy remarks that the story of Job is the story of the human struggle to understand. "Why do bad things happen to good people?" There are actually two endings to the Job story. One is where Job cannot reconcile his challenges for meaning and second, where Job is blessed again more abundantly. For Katy, it is about full acceptance of the human condition over which "I am powerless." We are called to give thanks and praise for life itself, always.

CHAPTER 10

Isaiah

Life in the Old Testament is war after war, hardship after hardship. One connecting idea are the men God chooses to bring words of wisdom to various kings and kings to be, the prophets. Isaiah is such a chosen person. He is on earth during the time of David.

In Isaiah 29, verse 7-8 it tells something of the properties of dreams. David's city of Ariel is about to be attacked, Isaiah offers this comfort. "Then the hordes of all the nations that fight against Ariel, that attack her and her fortress and besiege her, will be as it is with a dream, with a vision of the night – as when a hungry man dreams that he is eating, but he awakens, and his hunger remains; as a when a thirsty man dreams that he is drinking but he awakens faint, with his thirst unquenched. So it will be with the hordes of all the nations that fight against Mt. Zion."

Isaiah goes on to encourage the people to become more spiritual. In other words, although the enemy thinks he can accomplish winning the war, it is but a dream of his, a wish.

The verses remind me of what we, today, call compensation dreams. God wants us healthy and happy. If we do not have enough of something, like joy, in our lives, He will give it to us in dreams. We awake and the joy is gone but we are left knowing we need joy and a good idea of how to get that joy. That all depends on if we are practicing spirituality, writing and trying to understand our dream messages.

In fact, the next chapter, chapter 30 vs 1 says "Woe to the obstinate children, declares the Lord, to those who carry out plans that are not mine." You probably wonder how you should know God's plan for you and I say, write your dreams, and learn how to interpret them!

CHAPTER 11

Daniel and Joel

Daniel, in the Bible book carrying his name, was to become a part of King Nebuchadnezzar's court. These were all young, healthy, intelligent Israelites taken from Jerusalem, conquered by the King and were to be trained in the King's religion and culture.

Daniel and three of his friends, renamed Belteshazzar, Meshach, Shadrach, and Abednego, resolved not to defile themselves and their God by accepting the king's edict. They rebelled and would have to be accepted for what they were. As a reward, God gave them special knowledge and understanding of all literature and learning, and to Daniel He gave the gift of understanding visions and dreams of all kinds.

We all have dreams, our scientists have proven this. The thing to spend time learning is to interpret the dreams.

"Nebuchadnezzar had dreams, his mind was troubled and he could not sleep," it tells us in Chapter 2, verse 1. When we are troubled, our dreams are more intense. This is because someone much wiser than ourselves is trying to help us solve our problems. Once you understand the dream, gain the point of view your dreams wish you to change to, the dreams go away and your life changes forever for the better.

In verse nine we see that the king not only wants an interpretation of his dream but also wants someone wise enough to recall the dream for him. He is led to Daniel. Daniel tells the king that only God in heaven can reveal the mystery of the dream. A spark of God lives within each of us whether we believe it or not. We also can have access to the mystery of others dreams when we learn how to connect with this power within us.

For Daniel it meant praying before going to sleep for the Kings' dream and for the interpretation of the dream. The answer came in the night. Daniel was able to describe what the King saw, a statue of many mineral elements, gold, silver, iron, clay, bronze, and the rock, cut out by the hand not of the earth that rolls down and destroys the statute.

In the book of Daniel, it is a long story, summed up somewhat in the second chapter, verse 44-45. "In the time of those kings, the God of heaven will set up a kingdom that will never be destroyed, nor will it be left to other people. It will crush all those kingdoms (symbolized by the various minerals) and bring them to an end, but will itself (the rock) endure forever. This is the meaning of the rock, cut out of a mountain, but not by human hands, a rock that broke the iron, the bronze, the clay, the silver and the gold to pieces. The great God has shown the king what will take place in the future. The dream is true and the interpretation is trustworthy." The king was won over to belief, to knowing Daniels' God was the real God and changed his ways with regards to the God he worshipped, encouraging his people to do likewise.

If in my dream, I saw a statue made of all those minerals, one thing I might see different is that that statute is me. The various minerals are different parts of me, of my belief systems. When this stone crashes it, I could interpret that I am presenting myself wrongly. I'm not doing with my life what God wants me to do and I can be torn apart by that rock. I would awake knowing either I do nothing, let this happen or I begin to make changes. I would either go back to sleep with a prayer for knowledge or sit in meditative silence and wait to have a vision pointing me in either a different direction with my life or with a different understanding of a situation that is ongoing in my life. The head being gold might be saying something about my possibly over valued ego which I need to let go and spend more time listening to my creator.

You might wonder how I would know the statue is myself or yourself. Everything and everybody in a dream is probably a part of you. You could also be that rock, being rolled into the middle of a bad situation that you can change. This is told us once more in the next dream the king had. He dreamed of a beautiful tree that was tall enough to reach heaven, and gave refuge to all kinds of people and animals. A spirit came down from heaven in his dream and told him the tree must be cut down. Daniel reluctantly told the king his reign was ending, he must go live with the animals, eat grass; his royal authority was to be taken away from him. In chapter 4, verse 33; "He was driven away from people and ate grass like cattle. His body was drenched with the dew of heaven until his hair grew like the feathers of the eagle and his nails like the claws of a bird."

He lost his sanity until, one day, he praised God for the beauty around him and, then, God restored all to him. The king was humbled. The book of Daniel holds many dreams. In the seventh chapter, Daniel recalls one of his own dreams concerning four strange animals that frightened him greatly, Daniel turned to someone else for an interpretation.

Often we do not understand our own dreams. It is like the saying that we are too close to the subject, can't see the forest for the trees. It helps to share your dreams with someone else. They often see something in the dream that we cannot see. In dream groups, as many as ten or twenty explanations for the dream are given. Only the dreamer will know the truth because they will get that "aha" feeling of "why did I not think of that." God will touch their heart and they'll know the truth of the dream.

Interestingly, this dream of Daniels' may be the first mention of the coming of Jesus. In Daniel, chapter 7 verse 13, in the ending of the dream of Daniels, he tells us, "In my vision at night I looked, and there before me was one like a son of man, coming with the clouds of heaven." Verse 14; "He approached the Ancient of Days. He was given authority, glory and sovereign power; all peoples, nations and men of every language worshipped him. His dominion is an everlasting dominion that will not pass away and his kingdom will never be destroyed."

In keeping with the theme of this book, if it were my dream, or yours, the word cloud jumps out at me. In a cloud you can see nothing. Where in your life are you blinded to something or by something? In the dream you, a son of God, are coming out of the clouds. Things are becoming clearer for you. Understanding of a situation is finally coming to you and you will have power over your own future. Then again, everything and every person being you, are you the cloud? Are you blocking someone's future, perhaps a son or daughter, because you believe you are the only one with the right answer for their future?

It is a long dream and interpretation but well worth reading as the story of Daniel tells of the end of days which is really change, not end. The angel in his vision, in the very last chapter, Daniel 12 vs 13, tells Daniel; "As for you, go your way till the end (when the wars are over). You will rest, and then at the end of the days you will rise to receive your allotted inheritance." In other words, although a lot is said about the end of days; for you and me, life goes on.

Joel 2: verse 28-30
Repeated in Acts 2: verse 17-18
"And afterward, I will pour out my Spirit on all people.
Your sons and daughters will prophesy,
Your old men will dream dreams,
Your young men will see visions.
Even on my servants, both men and women,
I will pour out my Spirit in those days.
I will show wonders in the heavens and on the earth."

There are several places in the bible were we are warned against dreamers but nowhere does it say to not open that dialogue with your own creator. Beware people who try to influence you by their dreams. What is good for one may not be good for another, besides interpretation can vary from one's persons experience to the next. Spend some time and learn to interpret for yourself or in a group of trusted friends.

Other Possible Interpretations

I took the dream of the statute made of minerals to my dream group, we came up with other possible interpretations. If the statute dream was mine, perhaps false idols were being seen. Was I putting my own ego, my golden head, above searching for Gods' answer on decisions I make, like the money first or prestige or just being right? It might be a prediction of some difficult change coming and I'm being given a chance to emotionally prepare; going up a mountain is a challenge and could, therefore, be predicting a challenge or recommending a way of facing the challenge. Going up is good. The statute could represent the wealth of the world that can be gone in a minute, something or some attitude in your life that is frozen in time, be careful what you value. The interpretation that rang strongest with us was that change is coming, knocking down the image we adore. God is the rock and is bringing the change, we need to adjust.

Katy thinks the rock may be the process of evolution, spiritual, social and emotional. Ultimately evolution controls all from the big bang to the end of times. It is better to accept what we cannot change and with courage change with evolutions movement. The King is forced to recognize he is a creature, not a ruler over human affairs. Only the God of Evolution, Jesus' father has power over manifestation in human form, living, dying and rising to new life. We are called to do the same spiritually and emotionally. The rock, representing evolution causes move and change.

MARY'S VISIT TO ELIZABETH.

I·H·S

Elizabeth spake out with a loud voice, & said
Blessed art thou among women, &c.

Luke 1. v. 42.

Pub. by Hogg & Cº Paternoster row.

The Virgin Mary and her cousin had many
dreams before and after the birth of Jesus.

CHAPTER12

Matthew

The Dreams of Matthew are, perhaps the best known of the Christian world. Mary was engaged to Joseph, had never lain with him but was pregnant with a baby. Joseph was debating whether or not to go through with the marriage when he had a dream. In Matthew 1: verse 20 and 21, the story continues. "But after he had considered this, an angel of the Lord appeared to him in a dream and said, 'Joseph, son of David, do not be afraid to take Mary home as your wife, because what is conceived in her is from the Holy Spirit. She will give birth to a son, and you are to give him the name Jesus, because he will save his people from their sins." Joseph never questioned but obeyed.

On a note closer to our times, this is confirming the importance of always honoring your dream. Do something about it no matter how small. If the dreams encourage you to do something, perhaps exercise, change your diet, write your memoirs, do the best you can to follow this advice. God would never tell you to do anything that would be harmful to anyone.

In Chapter 2: verse 12, the child having been born, He is being honored by the wise men. "And having been warned in a dream not to go back to Herod, they returned to their country by another route." Verse 13 "When they had gone, an angel of the Lord appeared to Joseph in a dream. 'Get up,' he said, 'take the child and his mother and escape to Egypt. Stay there until I tell you, for Herod is going to search for the child to kill him.'" Verse 19, "After Herod died, an angel of the Lord appeared in a dream to Joseph in Egypt and said.' Get up, take the child and his mother and go to the land of Israel for those who are trying to take the child's life are dead." Verse 22 also mentions Joseph's dreams and his effort to save the life of the baby.

Your reaction is probably that this is Jesus, of course God and the angels would protect Him. You've heard this story since childhood. Wouldn't it be wonderful to have God, His angels, the saints and all the heavenly hosts watching out for you like that?

Well you do. We each have someone older, wiser, someone who knows our every deed and thought and still cares about our wellbeing. This person has been in my own dreams, giving me tips to heal, pushing me toward a better path than the one I was on, helping me to understand the things, situations, people who've hurt me and what to do about it.

Our creator has limitless ability to care for us. There's a reason for the hard to understand happenings of life. We learn these reasons through our dreams when we are ready for it, but, we need to keep the doors of communication open. This is the way God made us.

There is one more dream in the book of Matthew. In chapter 27, verse 19 is quite a different kind of dream. This takes place while Pilate is sitting in judgment about which of the men before him to crucify. "While Pilate was sitting on the Judge's seat, his wife sent him this message; 'Don't have anything to do with the innocent man, for I have suffered a great deal today in a dream because of him.'" Pilate listened to his wife and left the choice up to the crowd

CHRIST EXAMINED BY PILATE.

I·H·S

Then Pilate entered into the Judgment-hall again, & called Jefus, & faid unto him, Art thou ÿ King of ÿ Jews?

John XVIII. 33.

Pub. by Hogg & Cᵒ Paternoster row.

Jesus before Pilate.

In order to understand this as a dream lesson for all of us, we must put ourselves in the place of the one who had the dream, Pilate's wife. Our dreams are full of people and things. To understand what Spirit is trying to tell you, you must ask why the neighbor was in your dream when you know so many men, neighbors. The story could have included many alternatives but your neighbor was chosen because, perhaps you need to tell him something, or there is something in his personality that is also in yours.

When I know the person in my dream, I tell them about the dream, even if I need to make a joke out of it. You might be surprised at their reaction. If it is a personality thing, think are they impetuous? Perhaps you are about to make a rash decision.

Let's switch the story and suppose Pilate's wife was concerned about the whole situation. Suppose she asked her dreams for a message for her husband about Jesus. It works this way also. You can pray before going to sleep, perhaps write a note to God, and put it under your pillow before you go to sleep. Your dreams will often hold an answer. The dream may seem ridiculous but write it down. It will hold meaning later.

Katy says a circle of friends with whom you can share your dream is very important to gain perspective regarding the message of the dream. The dream is a revelation of God's truth for us. We want to understand fully the meaning of the dream.

Pilate's wife could not influence Pilate's decision making so he passed on it. By giving the decision to the crowd resulting in the torture and death of an innocent man. Pilate was responsible and his own decision deals a death he expected. We must listen for the truth of our dreams instead of listening to popular opinion.

CHAPTER 13

Acts

Acts 16, verse 9 it says "During the night Paul had a vision of a man of Macedonia standing and begging him, 'Come to Macedonia and help us.'"

Acts 18, verse 9, the Bible says, "One night the Lord spoke to Paul in a vision. Do not be afraid, keep on speaking, do not be silent, for I am with you and no one is going to attack and harm you, because I have many people in this city."

Acts 22, verse 17 Paul is speaking once more; "When I returned to Jerusalem and was praying at the temple, I fell into a trance and saw the Lord speaking. Quick!', He said to me. 'Leave Jerusalem immediately, because they will not accept your testimony about me.'"

Verse 21 reads "Go; I will send you far away to the gentiles."

Acts is all about the beginning of the Christian Church. Jesus is dead and has arisen. Paul and the other disciples travel far and wide to spread the good works Jesus had started. It appears Jesus guided them, sometimes through their dreams.

The purpose of this book is to find the lesson for us, individually, in each of these dreams. In this case, Paul had changed his life and was spreading the word of God. It makes sense that some agent of God would help him along the way. If these words are written down to tell you and me something, what can we take away from his experiences?

Would an agent, an angel, Jesus, God guide us along our life's path? These dreams remind me of the step by step process our creator used with me in my own dreams, pushing me to work with my dreams to co-create the life intended for me. While we may think we are getting the whole picture of our own path the first time we see a vision, we actually receive one small piece at a time. Like going to school, we need to know the ABC's before we can put words together. Finally maturity, and experience brings understanding.

When I began my spiritual walk, my dreams had me, a bookkeeper, writing funny stories, incidents in my life. I did it for fun, to see if I could. One day I made a friend, a college president, no less, who would meet me for lunch and edit my work. We met when we coincidently had adjoining booths at a health fair. She taught me the basics of writing. Gradually I was inspired in my dreams to write other things. A magazine publisher walked into my life and published my stories, then a television producer. I thought for sure this was my path. Life went on, things changed, I wrote and directed audience participation plays, tried my hand at young adult fiction; now dreams are my major focus. One little step at a time, I was led one more step at a time along my path of work for God, and He tells me that I'm not finished yet. There are more things to come, one that includes a mission I may be able to fulfill only after death. So I also learned that life goes on.

I believe this is what the night time visions of Paul are telling us. Jesus, or God, was leading him step by step to an ultimate goal. Paul followed his dreams without question. When you have a dream, honor it by doing something tied in with it. If your dream involves a truck, buy a small toy truck to keep on a shelf of dream symbols. Draw a picture of the dream, you might get a different view of the interpretation. If the dream has a food, either add or take it out of your diet as this may be a health related dream. If it has a profession you've not considered, try to make room for it as a hobby in your life. You are opening a door. Now wait and see what opportunities God brings to you.

One other aspect of Paul's dreams is the protection given him. It happens for us also. If you are headed down a path that is no good for you, you will get warnings, opportunities to change your mind about things, attitudes are all important. Sometimes the wars of your dreams indicate warring within yourself over which way to go. We get health warnings, by writing your dreams in a journal, you can track how many days between the sight of bugs crawling all over the hood of your car, your house, etc. and a case of actual flu. I had a certain relative with whom I could never do anything right for her. We argued constantly and one day, by tracking the dreams written in my journal, I realized I had been warned each time she would show up at my door. From then on, I was prepared and actually laughed to myself when she drove in the driveway. The disagreements did not bother me ever again and neither did the vision of snakes that would foretell she was coming. While we never became great friends (it takes two to change their minds and her attitude far predated me) I was the last one who sat at her bedside as she passed. You can learn from each person you meet.

Swarm of locusts.

CHAPTER 14

Revelations

Some people say that the Book of Revelations is one big dream and must be interpreted symbolically. According to the NIV Study Bible, there are four ways to interpret the Book of Revelation.

"The first group they call the Peterists who understand the book exclusively in terms of its first-century setting, claiming that most of its' events have already taken place.

The second group are the Historicists who take it as describing the long chain of events from Patmos to the end of history,

The third group are called the Futurists. They place the book primarily in the end of times.

The fourth is called the idealists who view it as symbolic pictures of such timeless truths as the victory of good over evil. We are encouraged to read it for its overall message and resist the temptation to become overly enamored with details."

I evidently read it as a young person, then dismissed it from my mind because I didn't want to think about the end of times and all those ugly images I didn't understand. As an adult, events in my life brought me a fresh understanding of the book. I came to see one of the stories as a part of my life. You might be touched by another of the stories. Each of our experiences are different and I came to see the

Bible as repeating themes in different ways in order to touch us much like our dreams do. If you have a powerful dream that you cannot interpret, it will repeat in a different setting in hopes of getting the message to mean something to you. In time, it will become what we call a recurring dream or even a nightmare.

The story of the locust came home to me when I was going through a hard time. It seemed I could not please anyone. There was a lot of animosity and one day I actually saw locust in my dream and realized that I could name each one of the locust in the story in Revelation.

That story is about my life and there were lessons to learn.

I found another story in the Book of Judges that also brought home to me that the Bible was talking to me personally on more than one level. I was at a dream conference and the morning speaker read an old poem by a 17th century man named Hakim. It was titled "The Ten Thousand Idiots Inside Me." It had made an impression on all of us because we were studying Carl Jungs' theories of the committee of souls inside each of us; the inner child, the old crone, the male, the female, the wise old man, etc. After lunch I went to my room, fell asleep and dreamed of the poem. On waking, I picked up the Bible and let it fall open to a chapter of Judges where a land was being taken away from one tribe and possibly given to another. A woman led the fight on one side and God told her to get her ten thousand soldiers to help her defend her position. It hit me, the poem. The story in the bible was not about yet another war, it was telling us, who could understand, we have to pull ourselves together, learn to make use of all the various parts buried deep inside us. There are so many similar stories because, like I said, we are all different and what opens me up to truth might not work with you.

Katy says "Many call the Bible the Living word of God. Carol is teaching how this living word reveals truth to each person through cultures, human experiences, feelings, the thoughts throughout time, two thousand years to the present time and into the future. Dreams and visions are 'My Book of Revelations' between God and my unique self.

CHAPTER 15

The New Oxford Annotated Bible

This Bible has several books not included in the bibles I was using or was familiar with but it had a much fuller index on dreams and became part of my research. The various books, written by different people seemed to have different views of dreams.

In the Wisdom of Solomon, chapter 18 verse 17-19, it is written; "At once nightmares, phantoms appalled them and unlooked for fears set upon them and as they flung themselves to the ground, one here, one there, they confessed the reason for their death. For the dreams that tormented them had taught them before they died so that they should not die ignorant of the reason they suffered."

There is a bit of wisdom in this passage and that is confessing the reason for their death. I've been doing dream interpretation for many years. People have been made to look at their attitudes and changed their attitude about things by doing their own dream work. We've learned a lot about ourselves that way and improved our lives. I have come to the conclusion that we are putting St. Peter, who guards the gates to heaven, out of a job. It was my understanding that we are judged on our lives before we enter the gates and told where to go based on how we've lived our lives.

Through dream work, we have been able to judge our own lives, properly, and make whatever changes are needed before we die. I envision a bunch of dream workers just sailing right by St. Peter.

In a Bible Book called Sirach, the author does not hold my views of dreams. In chapter 34, verses 1-8 the author has a lot of negative comments to say about people who believe in dreams, even calling us fools. He protects himself, in case he is wrong by saying in verse 6, something about the one exception is if the dream comes from the One Most High. He does leave a door open in case he's wrong.

Our friend, Katy, feels that the author of Sirach was trying to describe the difference between the dreams originating from the personal unconscious, the collective unconscious or from the Self (or God) within.

Other of these added books are very much filled with dreams. In 2 Esdras, chapter 14, verses 7 and 8, the author says "And now I say to you; lay up in your heart the signs that I have shown you, the dreams that you have seen, and the interpretations that you have heard." Do you keep a dream journal? I'll show you how a little later on.

In the book of 2 Maccabees, chapter 15, war is about to break out. Maccabee tried to arm his men with confidence in heavenly help. Verse 11 says, "He armed each of them not so much with confidence in shields and spears as with the inspiration of brave words, and he cheered them all by relating a dream. Verse 16 tells the dream. "In the dream, Jeremiah, the prophet of God stretched out his right hand and gave to Judas a golden sword, and as he gave it he addresses him thus; Take this holy sword, a gift from God, with which you will strike down your adversaries."

If it were my dream, I'd be looking within myself for my golden sword, possibly a talent with which I can win this war of life, or an attitude that needs polishing up.

PART TWO

Mechanics

CHAPTER 16

Mechanics of Remembering Dreams

If you have an interest in hearing what God might be telling you, start with a pad and pen next to your bed. Write the date on it and the words," I will remember my dreams." When you wake write down whatever was going through your mind, even if it was just that you had to make a bathroom run. Remembering your dreams must become a priority in your life. Talk about dreams, read about dreams. Honor your dreams. If you see or remember nothing but an elephant, draw a picture or find a toy elephant and start a symbol collection.

Dreams will gradually build just like exercising a muscle will grow the muscle. If no dreams are remembered that first night, do the same the next night. On a new page of the pad write the date and again, "I will remember my dreams."

When you do have a dream, do not try to understand it then, wait until tomorrow morning. Sometimes during the next day, something may happen that will remind you, "that was my dream."

Many people deny having dreams. Everyone dreams. Watch a baby as it sleeps, a puppy, a kitten. My belief is that this is the way God made us so that we can continue communicating with him after we've come to this earthly life. Sometimes through this method we also have access to where we were or what we did before this life. We are all connected much closer than we know. If my daughter is in my dreams, it is more likely to be about her than about me. My book "God Speaks in Dreams, Connect with Him and Each Other" will give you several examples of this.

Katy, our Jungian, remarks that if my daughter is in my dreams it may be about my inner child or be an aspect of myself reflected in my daughter that has been hiding in me.

Oft times, especially as a child, we have been so frightened of our dreams that we've somehow turned them off. Or, perhaps, a simple lack of interest in them has made us forget them. A family who discusses their dreams is a big help in understanding real spirituality.

On the other end of the spectrum, sometimes we are being bombarded with dreams and therefore picked up this book to see what someone else knew of dreams. Sometimes there is an increase in dream activity because of stress we are going through in our daily lives. This is the way it worked for me. So I picked up that first dream book to see what other people knew. The first line of the first book I picked up said that God was speaking to me. I have held this close to my heart ever since and the good that has come proves the statement true, to me.

CHAPTER 17

Starting a Dream Group

I've mentioned dream groups several times. I find this the best way to understand your dreams. A good size would be between 5 and 15 people who meet weekly. It becomes social, educational and intellectual.

Katy says that for her the group often takes a spiritual direction. We each learn something about God's presence in our own lives.

You need not share the meaning of your dream unless you want to. The person who had the dream is the only one to know the truth of the dream, you'll get that feeling of aha and why didn't I think of that? Sometimes we are just too close to a subject.

A person with a dream tells the dream. Key words can be written on a board or individuals can keep notes on tablet in their laps. The dream now belongs to the group and each person has a chance to say what the dream would mean if it were "my dream." In fact, it is best to begin your narrative with the words, "If it were my dream…" This way you are neither making judgments on the dreamer nor are you telling him or her how to live their life. An open mind and acceptance of all possibilities is necessary.

Since we believe God is trying to make our life better and there are the 139 mentions of dreams in the Bible, one would think churches would be leading the path of dream groups but mostly they happen in homes. In the late 1880's to 1920's the Unity Church had a dream section that turned into Silent Unity, a twenty-four hour prayer service. Charles and Myrtle Fillmore, the founders of Unity believed in going to God (headquarters) for answers to questions. This was in a time when people were dying like flies from TB, Myrtle, who contacted TB, was able to overcome it.

Dreams were one way they believed in having direct contact with God and getting answers to their problems. Their effort at making dreams part of their church found themselves overwhelmed with requests for dream interpretation. With the group situation, the group, in each individual church, can be led by themselves and hold the church together on a new, more spiritual level. I earned my degree in Dream Group Leadership from an Episcopalian Group. There is a publication named "The Rose" which lists many dream groups across the United States and a few in Europe. Dream groups are regularly held in Episcopalian Churches, according to this publication although I know a few others who also participate. There are a very few groups being held in prisons and my experience with this situation was a belief that understanding your dreams was the best, surest way to rehabilitation. In my days of leading such a group it changed their perception of the life and the doors open to them. It brought a sense of self-worth.

Hopefully the study of dreams will be more common once again, as in the days of the Bible.

CHAPTER 18

Are you Worthy?

Some people, I think, deep down have a feeling of unworthiness, of not being one that God would speak to. If you would study your dreams and meditations, you'd know differently. Let me tell you the story of Max Cleland. He published a piece about himself in the September/October 2012 issue of the Daily Word publication.

Max lost both legs and his right arm, very nearly his life, in Vietnam. After the war he overcame his difficulties and reached great success in his life of service and politics. He was named administrator of Veterans Affairs in 1977, served as the Georgia secretary of state, and was elected a United States Senator from Georgia in 1996. Today he is an author, "Strong at Broken Places" and "Heart of a Patriot," and serves as secretary of the American Battle Monuments Commission.

His biggest challenge when he had to rely on others for nearly everything was to let go and let God. Being a long time Daily Word reader, he relied on the words in it. He needed them and his friends to get through each day. He called it his daily dose of God, his sense of what's right with the world. I quote, "Ultimately we all come to a point when we've got a situation that we cannot handle ourselves. Through the grace of God and the help of friends we can become strong at the 'broken places." Max is a fan of Ernest Hemmingway and quotes him as saying,

"The world <u>does </u>break us. And once we are broken and at the point where tears are streaming down our faces, and we're crying out 'God help me,' once we get to that place and survive – you live another minute, another hour, you survive another day – when you are totally broken and have no place to go, God is there to strengthen and help you, and you get strong at the broken places."

Max goes on to say, "The real question is not so much, are we broken? Because the answer is yes. When we are disappointed, we're broken. When we experience loss, we're broken. When we grieve, we are broken. The question is, how do we get strong at the broken places?" His answer is through the grace of God and friends. I'd like to tell you more.

I love symbols, analogies and this story spoke to me of a life of broken bones symbolizing broken spirit. Its analogy strikes home with me. The break symbolizes the traumas of our childhood. The trauma heals; the bone becomes thicker, the spines of our lives become stronger.

But, sometimes they don't. Sometimes the memories haunt us, they become bad patterns in our lives, like depression, loneliness, dissatisfactions, anger. If the broken bones <u>don't</u> heal, the wound gets deeper. Does that explain a lot? We get better or we get bitter.

Max quotes Mark 9:24 where Jesus says "everything is possible for him who believes." A man with a dying son says, "I do believe: help me overcome my unbelief." To me belief in God is not the answer, knowing God would overcome any unbelief.

We believe, yet we don't know, so we have our doubts. Most often it's that I believe whatever great thing happened to some other people happened, but do not believe it would happen to me. Spirituality is not about a set of beliefs, not what you were taught growing up. Not even about the latest new way of thinking. Spirituality is all about knowing, connecting with Spirit yourself, getting answers for yourself. When you know you've done that, you've overcome your unbelief.

True spirituality is knowing; the surest way to know something is to communicate with your creator, your angels, and the entity who knows you best and loves you anyway. Go into meditation or ask before you go to sleep – ask why, then ask what do I do now or how can I heal this? My "broken bone" included a diagnosis of rheumatoid arthritis in my blood stream. After a year of working with God through my dreams, the disease was gone from my blood. My relationships changed for the better and I was on to a new vocation. The unbelief can manifest as an illness, a vocation, and\ or a relationship.

Going back to the broken bone, any person who makes you hurt holds power over you. Take the power out of your adversary's hands and be who you were meant to be. Those broken bones you hold may have come from some very nasty places. Every person has it in him\ herself to be a wonderful, special person. If you make me smile, you are special. You deserve more. Forget and forgive, find empathy for the ignorance of those who hurt you and don't let those things hurt you anymore. As long as you have fear, hate, hold a grudge, you've given up your power. Take your power back. Never ask why they did that to me, ask rather, why it bothers me. Fix it.

This is where forgiveness comes in, of the others and of yourself. You must come to understand those that were part of the very first wound. When you do, the heavy load you've been carrying will disappear.

Most all of us have broken bones somewhere in our lives. I found one of mine through an ugly pattern in my life. I'd get angry to the point of throwing up. After one such episode, I wanted it to be my last. I turned to Spirit. In meditation I asked was I wrong? Was I seeing things wrong? I was made to relive the argument again, plus another instance where the nausea outcome was the same.

Being on a first name basis with God, I rebelled, 'I know this.' I shouted in my mind. 'That's what I'm asking about!'

That night in my dreams I viewed a couple more instances. The next day in meditation there was another instance. The thing that kept me going, besides my desperation, was that these instances were being shown to me in chronological order, going back in time. It was a broken bone that never healed, it had only gotten worse. The series ended with my parents abandoning me to a set of grandparents I did not know, all because of their divorce, but I did not understand that I was at the beginning.

That day, as spirit so often works, an acquaintance dropped by and we got to talking about the dreams. I believed the abandonment didn't bother me – I ended up luckier than either of my parents and I often thanked my lucky stars – I carried no hate, so I thought. My friend pointed out that whatever I suffered made me who I was today and in some twisted way, I should thank my parents.

Now, thinking I'd reached the beginning of this pattern of unhappiness, I went back into meditation, I knew when the broken bone occurred so I asked, what do I do now to heal it? I didn't want to have those arguments anymore. The meditation took hold and I was shown those instances again, coming forward in time, only this time they showed me over reacting to whatever the situation was. Somewhat ashamed, I asked God what to do now. The answer was silence. I was either to figure it out myself or wait. I waited.

My parents, I now realized, did the best they knew how. I found empathy for them and wished I had done more for them before they passed. I realized that they were brought up a certain way, under circumstances I'd never really know but it all added to their ignorance in raising me.

I didn't have to ask forgiveness from the other various people. My attitude changed and those that mattered reacted differently to me.

The cracked bones –so to speak – now could finally heal. Emotionally I became stronger; I let slide things that had once offended me; I had more self-esteem in knowing why and how to heal.

In the symbolism of dream work, quite often you'll see a house which is all about your emotional self. If you catch your dreams, you'll see doors in that house opening that never opened before. You'll see whole rooms that you can fill the way you want them filled, new hobbies, love, job opportunities. You'll see these in waking life as well. I promise wonderful new beginnings. Those cracks and breaks in your spiritual bones will heal, the bone will get stronger, your strength will return.

And best of all – you'll now "know" your creator and that I Ie, She, It knows you – and loves you anyway!

Our friend, Katy, says that Spirituality is exploring the endless God – self within. Whatever you call this Life Force within, it will be ultimately experienced as love. Our dreams that emerge from the collective unconscious, or the world around us, provide us with metaphors for the mystery in which we live and move and have our being.

CHAPTER 19

Bringing Back Your Dreams

I can't recall being much interested in my dreams growing up. The only talk about dreams was from the grandmother who mostly raised me. Each morning she'd tell me about friends and relatives, long dead, who visited her during the night and how they'd reminisce about the days they grew up in. I was very much interested in those days. To give you some perspective, Gram had a part-time job playing the piano for the silent movies in the theater in the small Pennsylvania town she lived in. She also spent some time working the switchboard that connected people with their incoming telephone calls and dialed their out-going calls for them.

One night, she and Grandfather both woke to a pounding on their wooden headboard. The next morning, the phone operator on night duty the night before called to say someone had called at that same hour to say a relative had died. Gram and Grandfather believed it was the soul of that person stopping to say goodbye. Still I never thought of my own dreams. This was hers.

About mid-life, I found myself with a lot of stress which led to an illness found in my blood. I went into meditation and asked God why. Life had not been so good up to now and now I was looking forward to living the rest of it as a cripple. Visions took over, three that I could retain. I quickly wrote them in my journal and decided to put those visions into my life. They were talents, music, photography and writing. I used music to exercise to and began my first venture writing some funny things that happened. Photography had been what I thought of as a useless talent and had been on the verge of selling my camera. Because of the vision, I changed my mind. I knew the visions were not from my mind. Someone greater than I was sending me a message. I determined to catch my dreams like Gram had and see if God had more to tell me.

The key is to make dreams a priority in your life. Talk about them, read books about them, reread the dreams you've had and see if anything new comes to mind. If the dream had been a prediction, you won't know it until the event has occurred. Do not be frightened if something bad occurs in your dream. Even the gatherings around the death of someone close needs someone strong to help the others. God does not want us to be sick. Being forewarned eliminates a level of stress. Then, again, death in a dream is seldom death but rather a change in someone's life.

If something frightening is shown, it is never as bad as you have seen. You have an opportunity to change things, if you have been on the wrong path. Your attitude can make a huge difference in your reaction, being warned ahead of time, thinking about your possible reactions can change your attitude.

I put a pad and pencil next to my bed, wrote the date and the words "I will remember my dreams," on the first page. Nothing came through. The next night I did the same. I persisted, often writing just how I felt when I woke; sometimes one or two words were still in my head. Finally the dreams I could remember came. The first had me going across the Canadian border. The police stopped me and proceeded to search my car. They found illegal hams in my trunk. I got up, wrote it down and went back to sleep. The next morning, reading the dream, I had a good laugh. I was too heavy and did need to get the fat out of my trunk.

The dreams continued and with each I tried to make a change in my life according to what the dream said, or what I thought it said. Sometimes it was about what I thought about myself, what I thought others thought about me, what talents I had or did not have, what food I needed to add or take away from my body. Then opportunities walked in my door, so to speak. An opportunity came to write for money and it changed my life drastically. I was happy, within two years, the disease was gone from my blood.

The key, after so many years of ignoring my dreams is persistence. Like any muscle that has been let go, we need to exercise this dream muscle and make it stronger. You can do it also. God is waiting to communicate with you.

Review your dream journal periodically, keep a list of things you want changed about yourself on a back page and review it. Keep also a list of things for which you are grateful. You'll see changes come.

CHAPTER 20

Interpretation

No instance in your life is too small for God to take an interest. If it bothers you, it bothers Him. It has been said that someone older and wiser than us, someone who knows all about us and loves us anyway, wants the best for us, health, finances, career, and joy. This someone (I call God) speaks to us in dreams and meditation trying to change the way we think about a subject. I often had instances when a subject came up in my dreams that I didn't know bothered me. God knew and the outcome was rewarding.

Sometimes the scene in the dreams is straight forward, perhaps warning us of something to come. I often got predictions of things half way around the globe. I believe this happened to keep me interested in the dreams. It was neat, at least to my way of thinking, to have advance knowledge of something even though there was nothing I could do about it.

The majority of dreams, however, need interpreting. If I were to tell you to pick up something, for instance, you could easily ignore me. If the scene you see is of that same something containing something dangerous to yourself, you would find a way to get it removed. It's the emotions that move us.

Another suggestion I strongly make is to study Carl Jung. You will learn to discern your male and female energies or sides, your shadow (which can be good or bad) and other energies within you like the crone, the wise man, the mother or father energy, and how God may be using them to tell you something.

Another way to interpret a dream is to become an image in the dream. This was taught to me by Dr. Robert Hoss, another dream researcher and past president of the Association of the Study of Dreams (IASD). Ask yourself questions. Become the image. After each image, I'll give you a few common interpretations from other dream symbol books and then show you what can happen when you become the image.

Bones; Do you have a bone to pick with someone? It can mean strength and your ability to carry your load, bare bones = just give the facts. If you go the route of asking yourself questions as if you are those bones, it might go like this. First describe yourself. If you have ever seen a skeleton you know what I am. My purpose is to hold the flesh and organs of a living body together but as yet, I don't have a body or through my actions I have lost who I am supposed to be. What I like about myself is that I have the potential to be a body or to be a teaching tool. What my biggest fear is that I'll be forgotten. My biggest wish is that I can find out what my purpose is and fulfill that purpose, be useful. See box.

If I were a dog, a bone might be my greatest treasure. What do you treasure?

Box; can mean a boxed or closed-in feeling, unfortunately you are living in the limits of your surroundings, boundaries, and a block to your progress or it can be a gift. Everything in the dream being you, I once heard a dream in a prison class where the dreamer had dreamed of walking through the woods and finding a box that had the bare bones of a person spilling out. Her first instinct was to fold the bones back into the box and hide the box. End of dream. That box and those bones was the situation she had gotten herself into. She is trapped in a box of a cell. Her worth may be that of a bunch of old bones. The woods represented all the issues in her life. Now, in the box of a cell, she could straighten herself out, pack the old dead self away and start working on a new self.

Chicken legs; Legs denote the ability to stand up for one's own rights. Being chicken legs, and if the dream were mine, I would look to where in my life I lack that ability. The dreamer was to insert raw chicken legs into plastic bags. Someone told her that she was doing it wrong. We tried to find meaning within the dream group but this had us stumped. We asked ourselves questions like, were her legs strong enough to carry her body? She seemed to have no problem in that area. We let the dream go and found her with a bad cold or flu the next week. One of the dream group members, living close by, fed her chicken soup and other beverages. She recovered and we decided the dream was a warning this was in her future.

Cookie; Even the most normal dream, like one of the past, will hold something unusual. This dream had me eating cookies. I tried talking to the cookie as if I was the cookie. I described myself as round and chocolate chip. My purpose in life, so I told myself, was to be eaten. What did I not like about that was the short life I would have. What I liked about being a chocolate chip cookie was the joy I was able to bring to others. My biggest fear was being dropped on the floor and crushed under someone's feet. Hmmm. Was there somewhere in my life where this was a real fear? The greatest joy I had as a cookie was wishing I could last forever and bring more people joy. My answer to the dream was to step out of my circle and see where I might help someone else.

Doors; Doors in a dream are an invitation to something new. Go back into the dream and open that door. You have a new opportunity to bring something better into your life, make room for something you always wanted to do. Watch your life for a chance at something that will increase your good health, your joy, etc. In a dream, a person is walking through a house and comes to a closed door. If I take the part of the door, I first describe myself. I'm a plain door inside a house. My purpose is to lead someone into another space, a space they have never been. What I like about being a door is that I can swing open or shut, I offer a different view of things. What I don't like, in this dream, the person is not making use of me. My biggest wish is that he or she would open me and see the space in their life that they can fill any way they want. Or they find antiques worth a lot of money and it would solve their financial problems.

Egg; The common interpretation for an egg is new growth or opportunity. Talking to the dreamer as the egg can open other doors of understanding. Another lady, not in prison, dreamed of holding an egg with a piece of shell missing. The people around her spoke of throwing it away, frying it, using it anyway. She thought of herself as the egg, like thousands of other eggs only with that one tender, vulnerable spot. Everyone was telling her what to do. If she could do anything she wanted she would hatch into a real bird and fly away. This held great meaning for her life.

Frog; Can be an ancient symbol of something unclean in your life, or your prince that needs kissing is about to make an entrance in your life. It can be a play on words such as being a little frog in a big pond. One of the most common ways to decipher your dream, after writing it, is to imagine yourself as every person and everything contained in the dream. I once heard a dream where a lady walked into a child's bedroom that had wall paper full of frogs. There was a toy frog on the floor. As she thought of herself as the toy frog, she was glad she was not like the rubber stamped ones on the paper and that she could move around and be held by the child. If she were the child, she'd be glad when she and the frog became grown up, bringing freedom, clearer thinking, less of the sameness of that room, more of the ability to leave the room. It meant a lot to her to think she could think for herself and not be a copy of someone else – or sit on the walls like someone else expected of her.

Gold: There was a lot of the color gold in my dream and my mind went to the metal, gold. Gold must be mined and, to me, something good is being formed, dug out of my unconscious. Good days are ahead.

Gutter: A common meaning applied to the vision of a gutter is the saying about being stuck in a bad place. To describe myself, I am a half pipe that goes around a house just below the roof. My purpose in life is to catch the rain and funnel it to the corners of the house. What I don't like about being a gutter is that often I am forgotten, not kept clean of leaves, etc. My biggest fear, if I were the gutter, is the freezing ice cycles that can drag me down in the winter. My biggest wish is that I could add to the beauty of the house and be attended faithfully and that people would appreciate the job that I do. In all, if you had this dream, is there some area of your life where you would like more appreciation for what you do?

Leaves, dead; Old issues not dead but not forgotten. Sweep them away. The dream that prompted this addition was that I was going swimming in the pool and found the bottom of the pool thick of dirty, dead leaves. To describe myself, I'd first have to say I was a useless old leaf, or perhaps an issue in my life that was dirtying my life. This must be cleaned up in order to continue my activities in a pleasant manner. My purpose, as an old leaf is too keep alive old memories of things best cleaned up and forgotten. What I don't like about being a dead leaf is that I take up room in the pool of this small life that could be free of old issues, memories. Someone could clean me up and have a more fun, healthy, and successful life. What I like about these old leaves is the ability to relive the past and perhaps learn something from them. My biggest fear, though, is in the remembering, keeping these issues alive. It is best to defeat them, not let them become a pattern in my life. My biggest wish is to have a clean pool, a clean emotional and spiritual place to rest my heart.

Lizard; perhaps something to fear; the little lizards in Florida are a delight to most; if a child catches them by the tail, the tail will release and grow back. Perhaps we have something we need to let go. I once dreamed of watching a small lizard climbing up the inside of a window pane in my kitchen. First I described myself as the lizard which was small compared to the big world outside that window. I liked that I could climb up (up is good) and maneuver to see more and more. That is life as our maturity grows. What I did not like was being trapped inside. Where in my life did I feel trapped? My biggest fear was falling. If I could have anything in the world, as that lizard, it was to be outside, free and enjoying Gods' world more than I was. In fact, the dream ended with a man gently taking the lizard outside and letting it loose. The man, my masculine side, would show me how to solve my problems. One of my wishes will soon come true.

Then I did the same with the other images and people in that dream. It gave me a much clearer view of who I really was and what I needed from life.

A man; If a man you know is in your dream, you must ask why him, why not one of the many other men you know? Look at his personality. Your clue may lie there. If he is shy, silent, industrious, look to those traits in yourself. Then look at his place in the dream. Is his actions in the dream something you should think about for your own life?

Person (see man); If someone you know is in your dream, you might contact this person and tell him the dream. It may be a message for that person instead of for you.

Rock: Common interpretations include being changeless, solid, unbending, barrier, difficulty. A women in my dream group dreamed of walking a path between high mountains, going up (that's important) when she sees a rock that is shiny, flat on one side like a grave marker but with no writing. We decided on the stone as the odd object in the dream and she became the rock. She said I'm sitting by the side of the road. (Did she feel this way in waking life, a watcher rather than a partaker?) I can see lots of feet moving around me and a river flowing by with boats of people going somewhere. One side of me is polished marble or granite with beautiful designs. The other side of me is just a natural rock. As for a purpose, I seem to be a marker although there are no words on me. I don't like not being aware of my purpose in life. I like that I am solid and strong. My biggest fear is nobody stopping to see me. My greatest wish is they see that although I am just a rough stone on one side, they will realize my inner beauty and realize they also have inner beauty. This is the message I'd like to bring to everyone.

Vehicles; A car can be your very personal ride through life. One important question – are you in the drivers' seat? A bus may be talking of your place in your community, of your job, your friends, family. In my own dreams I was once in the backseat of a convertible, my son and his girlfriend whom I loved were in the front. So it was about their life, not mine. The car was going backward over a cliff. In order to interpret it, I became the car, I'm not in control. The relationship is going backwards and may die at the bottom of the cliff. My wishes did not matter in this instance. In life, the relationship did end.

Along the same line, a lady in my dream group dreamed of taking a trip on a hay wagon. She'd never been on one. So we asked her to try to think like this hay wagon in her dream. She described herself as a flat wagon pulled by a tractor. Her purpose was after the harvest of hay or straw, she'd be loaded for the care and feeding of farm animals. She says she'd be rolled out and bales of hay would be loaded on her. What she liked about being the hay wagon was that she was the most important piece of equipment on the farm. There was not a farm without one. What she did not like was sitting in a corner alone most of the time. Her biggest fear was that they'd never need her. Her biggest wish was to be more useful. She could see a lot of her life as she was living it in these statements and ideas came to get her biggest wish.

War; A common interpretation might be a need to forgive yourself for something. If a war is raging around you in your dreams, what kind of a war is going on in your home life, your work life, or a decision you're trying to make? An attitude may be causing you trouble even though you don't see it that way. Dream dictionaries are helpful but can also be a hindrance. They may stop you from thinking of other reasons for a symbol to be in your dream.

Bibles Used In This Study
The King James Version – Red Letter Edition
The New King James Version
The NIV Study Bible
The New Oxford Annotated Bible